CAJUN ALPHABET

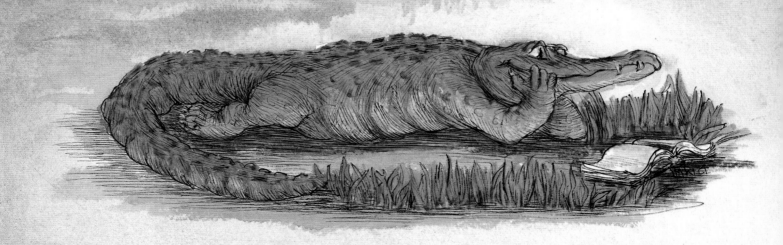

CAJUN ALPHABET

FULL-COLOR EDITION

**Written and Illustrated by
JAMES RICE**

**The Illustrator of
CAJUN NIGHT BEFORE CHRISTMAS**

PELICAN PUBLISHING COMPANY
Gretna 1991

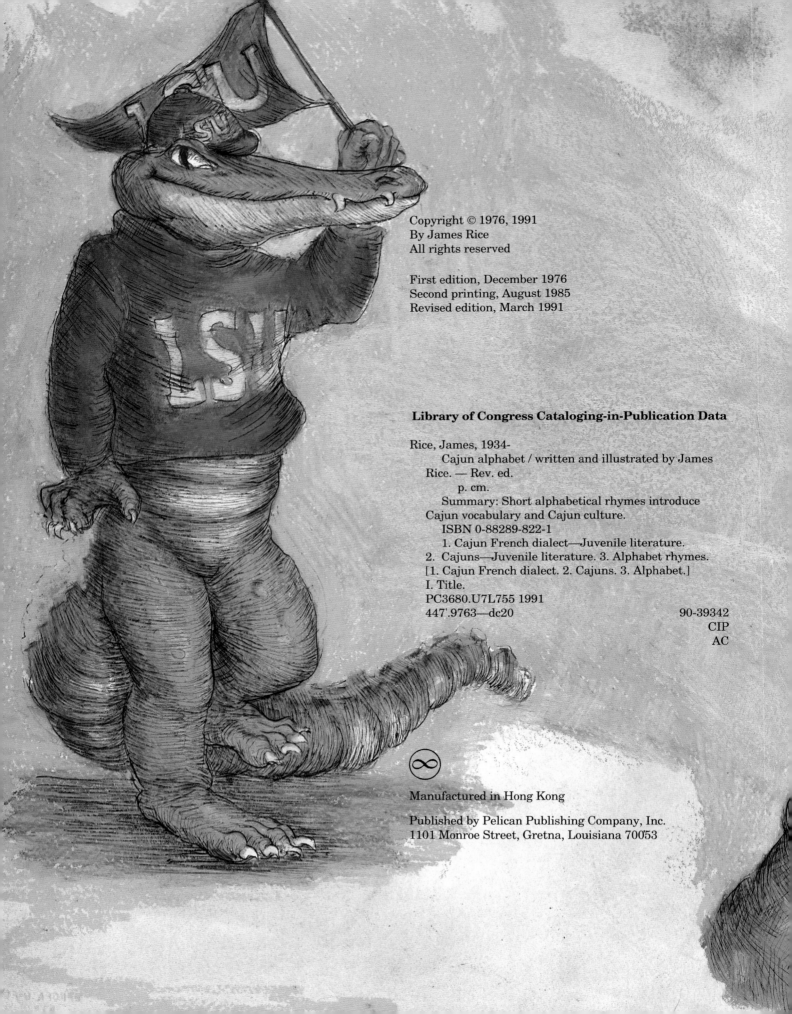

First edition, December 1976
Second printing, August 1985
Revised edition, March 1991

Library of Congress Cataloging-in-Publication Data

Rice, James, 1934-
    Cajun alphabet / written and illustrated by James
Rice. — Rev. ed.
        p. cm.
    Summary: Short alphabetical rhymes introduce
Cajun vocabulary and Cajun culture.
    ISBN 0-88289-822-1
    1. Cajun French dialect—Juvenile literature.
2. Cajuns—Juvenile literature. 3. Alphabet rhymes.
[1. Cajun French dialect. 2. Cajuns. 3. Alphabet.]
I. Title.
PC3680.U7L755 1991
447'.9763—dc20   90-39342
                                                         CIP
                                                          AC

Manufactured in Hong Kong

Published by Pelican Publishing Company, Inc.
1101 Monroe Street, Gretna, Louisiana 70053

Gaston decided he needed an education. To enter a university he either had to know the alphabet or play football. He could not find a football uniform that would fit, so he got an alphabet book instead. He opened a page and started to read.

is *Acadia,*
A place far away,
The Cajuns were exiled
To the bayou to stay.

A is *ami,*
A friend good and true,
When hard times come on
You'll find there are few.

A is *amour,*
An expression of love,
Your heart flutter flutters
Like the wings of a dove.

A is *animaux*,
  Every farm has a few,
Chien, vache, des poulets,
  Un cheval, et minon.

A is *alligator,*
    Gaston is one,
He goes sur l'terre tremblée,
    The bayou's his home.

A is *aigrette,*
    The swamp is his place,
He glides over treetops,
    His form is pure grace.

A is *au revoir,*
    So long, not goodbye,
I'll see you demain
    C'est amitié, you and I.

is *battoir*,
    For the washing of clothes,
They all will be cleaner
    If they last through the
blows.

B is *barbue*,
    A fine whiskered fish,
You broil him or fry him,
    There's no tastier dish.

B is *bayou,*
    With no current to see,
There's a pirogue tied up
    To a tall cypress knee.

B is *batture,*
    A backwater pool,
Where water unmoving
    Stands silent and cool.

B is *baire,*
Le maringouin to repel,
If he gets through to bite you,
It's hard to sleep well.

B is *bébé,*
A joy to behold,
Wrap him in blankets,
Don't let him get cold.

B is *bebelle,*
Pour l'enfant a toy,
A nice petite plaything
For a girl or a boy.

B is *bouré*,
    An old Cajun game,
When purses are empty,
    It's often to blame.

C is *courting tacky,*
  A horse that performs
Pour la belle amoureuse
  With a million odd charms.

C is *cochon,*
  A fat lazy hog,
He eats kitchen scraps
  And lies in a bog.

C is *chantez*,
    When you carry a tune,
A gay Cajun song
    That ends all too soon.

C is *courir du Mardi Gras,*
    Mardi Gras on the run,
Far out on the prairie,
    There's no greater fun.

C is *Catahoula hound*
    With yeux du pâle bleu,
He chases cochons
    Near the winding bayou.

C is *Cajun,*
Le meilleur in the land,
If you're ever in trouble,
He'll give you a hand.

C is *choc,*
    A bird black as coal,
To strip bare your cornfield
    Is always his goal.

C is *cuite,*
    The syrup so thick,
It sticks to the ladle,
    It's tasty to lick.

C is *couteau de cannes*
    To cut the tall cane,
Then bale it and haul it
And sell it for gain.

C is *chat sauvage,*
    His tail grows so short,
He's wild and ill-tempered,
    Not one to cavort.

C is *chêne vert,*
    Grandest tree on the bayou,
With leaves over an arpent
    It will shade me and you.

C is *charivari*
    For the fine bride and groom,
Some good-natured hazing
    After jumping the broom.

C is *Créole,*
    Dark hair and fair skin,
Royal French and pure Spanish
    Are claimed as their kin.

C is *chalon,*
   A moving boat-store,
Bringing groceries and gossip
   To all those on shore.

C is *crevi,*
   A crawfish so small,
You'll need forty douzaine
   If you plan to feed all.

D is *daim,*
　　He seeks the high ground,
He flies on winged feet
　　At the hint of a sound.

D is *drague,*
　　To catch a few fish,
You put bait on the hooks
　　And sit back and wish.

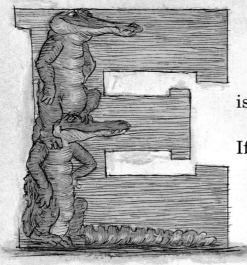

E is *étouffée*,
 It's better than stew,
If I eat my fill,
 There'll be none for you.

E is *écoute*,
 If you open your ear,
Then all of the sounds
 Are perfectly clear.

E is *éronce*,
 A blackberry bush,
Pick slow and be careful,
 It'll scratch if you rush.

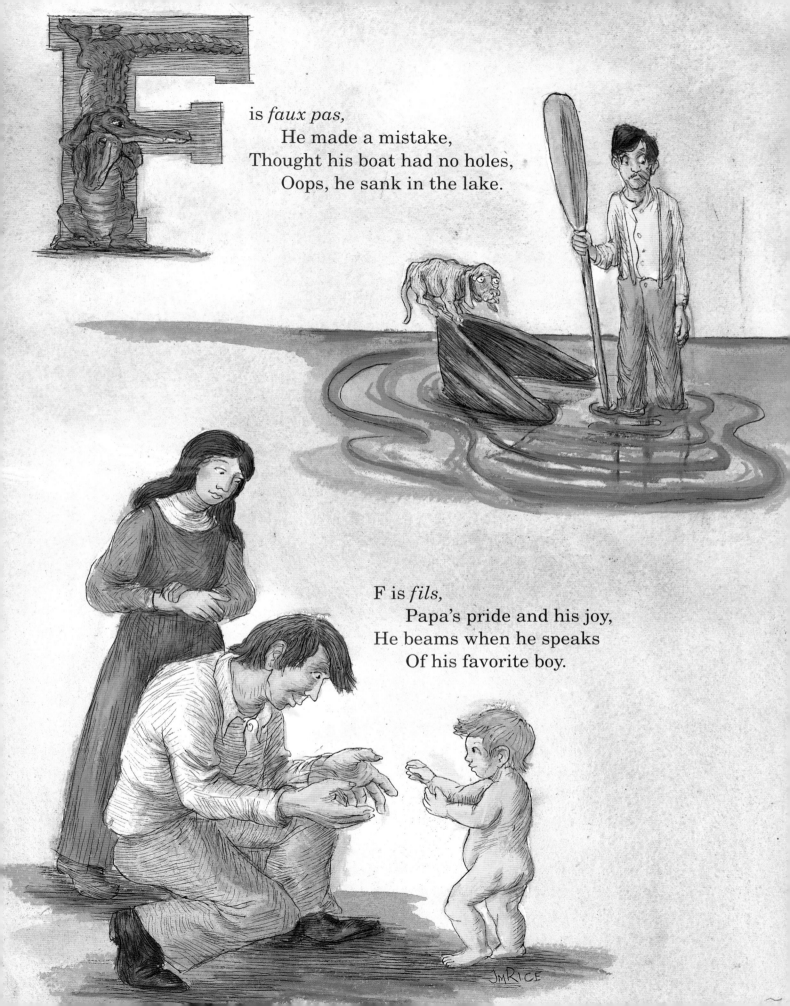

F is *faux pas*,
　　He made a mistake,
Thought his boat had no holes,
　　Oops, he sank in the lake.

F is *fils*,
　　Papa's pride and his joy,
He beams when he speaks
　　Of his favorite boy.

F is *fais do do*,
    A fine Cajun dance,
It'll last until morning,
    Go, if you've got the chance.

F is *forgeron*
    With arms like hard steel,
He'll shoe your cheval
    Or respoke your wheel.

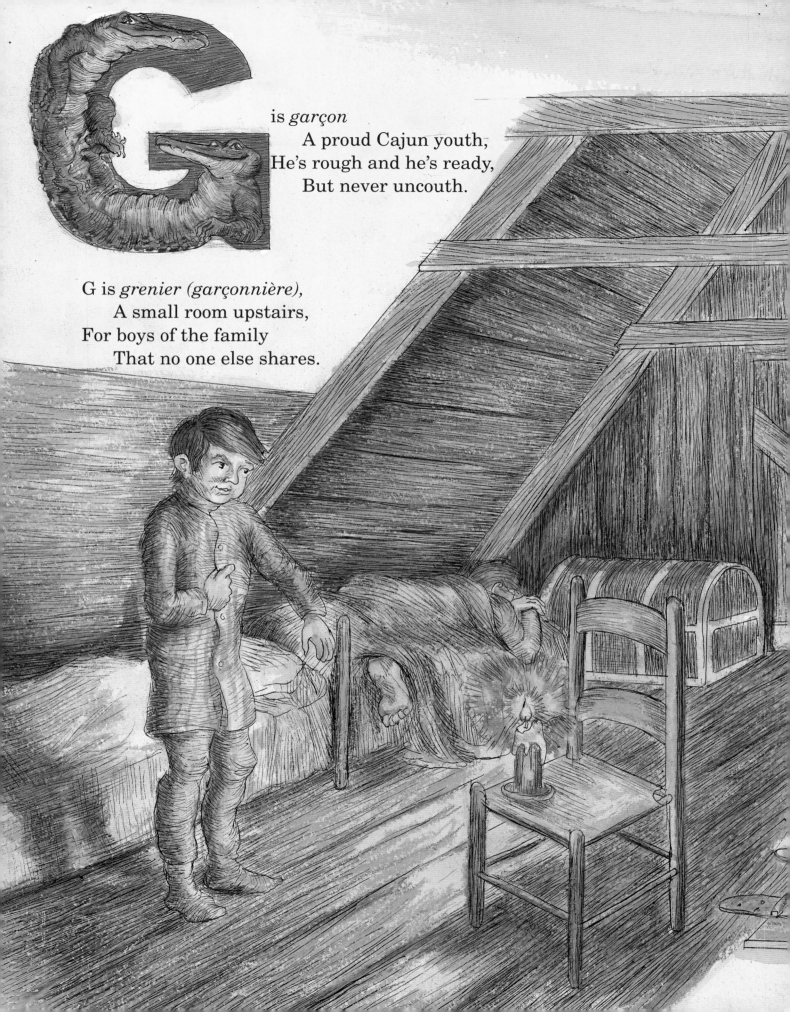

G is *garçon*
  A proud Cajun youth,
He's rough and he's ready,
  But never uncouth.

G is *grenier (garçonnière)*,
  A small room upstairs,
For boys of the family
  That no one else shares.

G is *galerie*,
    A porch and much more,
Where friendly folk gather
    In front of the door.

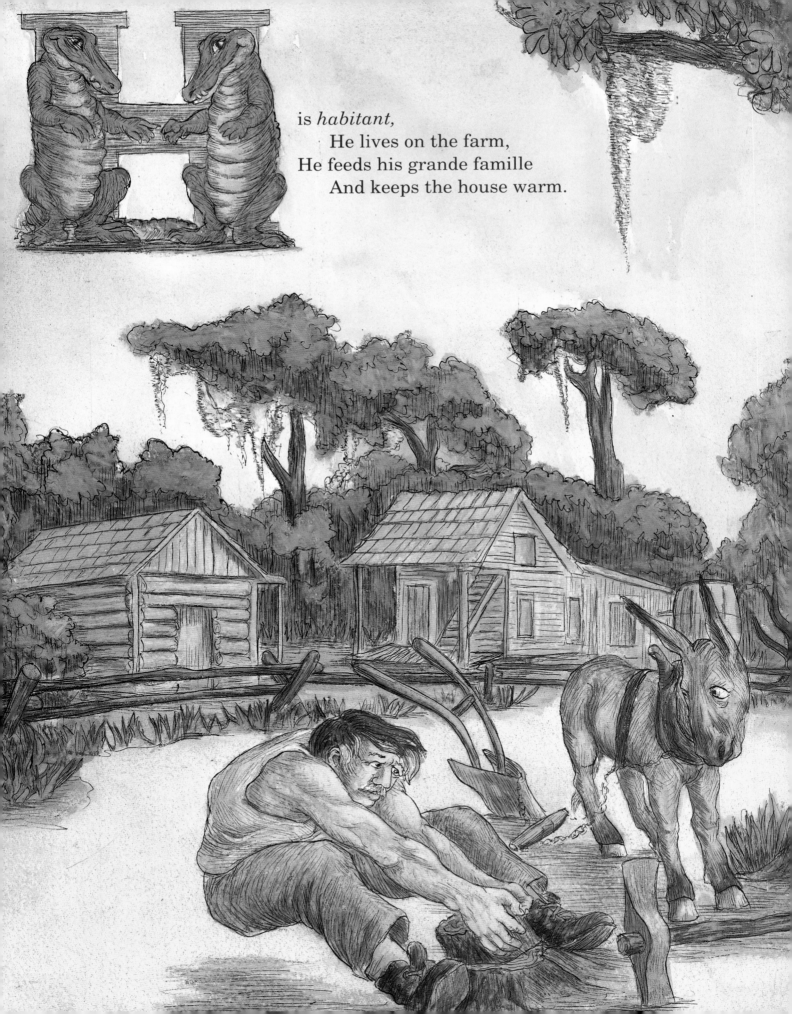

is *habitant*,
He lives on the farm,
He feeds his grande famille
And keeps the house warm.

H is *hibou,*
　　Just a swoosh in the night,
He hunts in the darkness
　　And stays out of sight.

H is *huracan*,
  With wind and with rain,
It blows through the marshes
  And levels l'terrain.

is *ingénieur*,
    He steers the great boat,
Up la grande rivière
    He keeps it afloat.

I is for *île d'chêne*,
    Thick oaks surrounded by land—
Islands out on the prairie
    Untouched by a human hand.

I is *igloo*,
    You'll not find one here,
You never will see one
    In the Southland I fear.

I is *ilet,*
 A full city square,
With banquettes et maisons,
 There's much to compare.

is *jambalaya,*
A fine Cajun dish,
Where good food is common,
It's all one could wish.

J is *joie de vivre,*
Pure joy of life,
A good Cajun has it
Through good times and strife.

J is *jeremiads,*
A bad stomachache,
From too much indulgence
In candy and cake.

is *korusse,*
    He starts a new day,
He crows before sunrise
    And drives sleep away.

K is *kerchief*
    Mama wears on her head,
She'll not remove it
    Till she's ready for bed.

L is *lagniappe*
    To round out the trade,
    Something extra pitched in
    And no charge is made.

is *mousse*,
    It's draped from the tree,
It's lonely and sad
    But lovely to see.

M is *moccasin*,
    His mouth lined with cotton,
If he sinks his fangs in you,
    It will make you feel rotten.

M is *muskrat*,
    He lives in the marsh,
With traps in the paths
    His life is so harsh.

M is *Mardi Gras*
    With a laugh and a song,
It's also Fat Tuesday
    With parades all day long.

M is *marchand*,
  He tends to the store,
He'll sell you most anything
  If it's out on the floor.

is *nanane,*
    A small piece of candy,
If you've a sweet tooth,
    Then keep a box handy.

N is *nainaine,*
    One's own dear godmother,
She'll always be near you,
    Greater love hath no other

is *ouanga*,
To cast off the spell
Of witches' bad voodoo,
How she'll not tell.

O is *ouaouaron*,
His croak fills the air,
He leaps sur grandes jambes,
He has a strong pair.

P is *pirogue,*
　　It floats on a dew
Or muddy swamp water
　　That never is blue.

P is *péniche,*
　　A flat-bottomed boat,
They'll harvest the moss,
　　Loading all they can float.

P is *pique-bois,*
　　He wears a red hat,
He makes holes in tree trunks,
　　Going rat-a-tat-tat.

P is *paillasse,*
　　A jovial clown,
He's always laughing,
　　He never will frown.

P is *pain,*
　　A loaf long and thin,
So tasty when hot,
　　It's almost a sin.

P is *poule d'eau*,
    A bird or a fish,
The best of two worlds,
    It's all he could wish.

P is *papillon*
    With colorful wings,
From flower to flower,
    Sweet pollen he brings.

is *quai*
        To tie up the boat,
If you don't make it fast,
        Away it will float.

Q is *queue de rat*
        Like the tail of a cat,
It's tall, thin, and furry,
        Can grass grow like that?

R is *rat de bois.*
　　He uses his head,
When he senses danger,
　　He sometimes plays dead.

R is *remède,*
　　A cure for the ill,
You make it at home,
　　No doctor, no bill.

R is *roux,*
　　A base for the sauce,
With onions and flour,
　　No flavor is lost.

R is *ravat,*
　　A pesky brown bug,
He'll hide in your wallboards
　　Or under your rug.

S is *shrimp boat*
    With nets on its side,
When gulf shrimp are running,
    It sails with the tide.

S is *sous bois*,
    So tangled and thick,
It is hard to discover,
    The right path to pick.

S is *sucrerie,*
    Where sugar is made
From cane that grows thick
    And casts a long shade.

S is *savane*
    To pasture the cow,
Tall grass and cool water
    Will fatten her now.

S is *sauter l'balai*,
    It's jumping the broom,
When the father's away,
    It'll join bride and groom.

S is *sacamite*,
    Made from ground corn,
I know you will like it
    As sure as you're born.

is *tante,*
>   She's sister to Pa,
> She married my nonc,
>   Who's brother to Ma.

T is *traînasse,*
>   A trail for the pirogue,
> To cut through the marsh-
> land
>   Where tall grasses grow.

T is *ti'fer,*
    To help keep a tune,
   With fiddles and guitars,
    They'll be playing soon.

T is *tablette,*
     A small wooden shelf,
It's outside the window,
     Papa built it himself.

T is *tamponne,*
     A woman too fat,
Rich food and soft living
     Have made her like that.

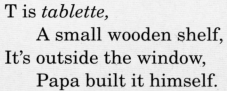

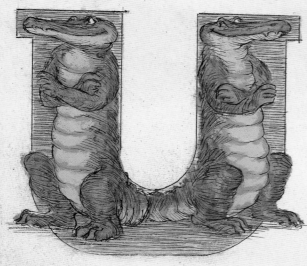

is *ustensile*,
  To set on the coals
And hold all the cuisine,
  Barbue, gumbo, and rolls.

is *vieille*,
    An old lady or wife,
A faithful companion,
    She'll remain so for life.

V is *voisin*,
    A neighbor and friend,
His very last dollar
    He gladly will lend.

W is *waguine*
    To haul in the crop,
Don't pile it too high
    Or something will drop.

W is *willow,*
    So dreamy and sad,
It'll make a cool shade
    For a tired, weary lad.

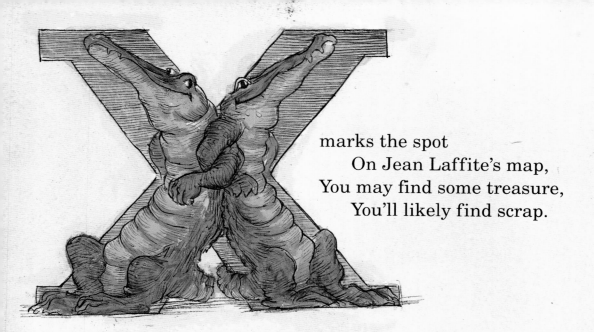

marks the spot
  On Jean Laffite's map,
You may find some treasure,
  You'll likely find scrap.

is *yam*
     To cook with the possum,
If you eat it with riz,
     Then red cheeks will blossom.

Y is *yeux,*
     Du brun, bleu, or gris,
They can invite you near
     Or chase you away.

is *zapote*,
  A hard wooden shoe,
Stuff it with moss
  To make it fit true.

Z is *zombi,*
    A frightful, mean ghost,
If ever you cross him,
    He'll burn you to toast.

Now you know your ABCs,
As every Cajun should.
You can talk with fluent ease,
They'll understand you good.